BOUNCE
BACK

A RESILIENCE GUIDE TO HELP
WOMEN TRANSITION FROM
STRUGGLE TO SUCCESS

WRITTEN BY

T'NESHEIA DAVIS

Published by Live Limitless Authors Academy & Publishing Co.

Publishing@sierrarainge.com

T'nesheia Davis Contact Information:

Email: taidaviscollectionproducts@gmail.com

Website: www.taidaviscollection.com

Printed in the United States of America

Cover Design by: Adam I. Wade

Cover Photo by: Nathan Pearcy

ISBN: 978-1-952903-06-9

Library of Congress Number: 2021903938

DEDICATION

Noah Davis & Nyla Davis

for being my reasons why I keep going so hard

BOUNCE BACK

ACKNOWLEDGEMENTS

I would like to thank God first and foremost for taking me on the journey to still be alive to share my testimony to help others that may be struggling. I want to send a special thank you Dr. Jitendra Sharma for being the only doctor on call to be able to perform that type of life saving procedure to remove the blood clot from my brain. I want to thank my children Noah and Nyla Davis for giving me so many reasons why I wanted to live, to not give up and keep pressing forward, not settling and continue to keep building generational wealth. To my husband, my best friend Demarice Davis, thank you for being there for me and being super supportive in anything I set my mind to. You never allowed me to give up. You were one of my biggest cheerleaders through all of my failures and wins. Thank you for being a great father and supportive husband. To my mother Lucille Moore, words can not express how thankful I am to you for instilling these values and life long skills in me from a little girl that shaped and formed me into the woman I am today. You have taught me so much on how to navigate through this thing called life and have been there every step of the way to let me know that I can do anything I put my mind to. You have always believed in me when no one else did.

TABLE OF CONTENTS

Dedication iii

Acknowledgements v

Table of Contents vii

Introduction 1

Chapter 1: The Adversity Advantage 7

Chapter 2: Resilience, Recovery & Redemption.............. 19

Chapter 3: Living your Truth 29

Chapter 4: Finding Your Purpose through alignment,
visualization and materialization 33

Chapter 4: The God-Given Vision.................................... 37

Chapter 6: Abandon your Comfort Zone 43

Chapter 7: Processing Grief 51

Chapter 8: Weight Loss.. 61

Chapter 9: Bounce back from divorce or a bad relationship 69

Chapter 10: Stories of women who have experienced a bounce back 73

Summary 81

About the Author 83

INTRODUCTION

Growing up in a small town. Birmingham, Al (Ensley) I didn't know any CEO's or anyone who aspired to be one except my mom. I watched my mom work her fingers to the bone day in and day out. She always instilled in me as a little girl "be your own boss" so that you don't have to work and put up with BS from these jobs like I did. As I grew older and wiser, those words started to make more sense to me. I went to cosmetology school at 18 years old. I knew that was one way I could be my own boss. I was never afraid to go after what I wanted, even if that meant failure. At the same time, I didn't know what it meant to become a CEO or what a CEO looked like. All I knew was that I wanted to be one, one day. My mom decided that she wanted me to go to cosmetology school to make my dream happen. She has always wanted me to be an entrepreneur though at the times I really didn't know what that meant as a kid. She signed me up to enroll at Dudley Cosmetology University in Kernersville, NC. For a moment I was terrified at the thought of leaving home at such a young age. I had never been away from my home except maybe a sleepover at a friends house from time to time. The day I went to school my mom and step dad stayed with me for a week to help set up my new apartment and helped me to get acquainted with my new room mate who I was very excited to meet. We were from the same region. She was from Mississippi and I was from Alabama. After my mom and stepdad left. I cried for days maybe even weeks until I was able to adjust to this new thing called life that I was experiencing on my own for the first time.

I was excited to assert a new level of independence but this new version of my life came with its challenges. There were plenty of times where I would call home and tell my mom to come get me because I didn't want to do it anymore; even though there were several moments that I wanted to pack up and return to my comfort zone, I never gave up. That experience alone taught me so much about life and about myself that I began to crave more of my independence and with that my life continued to evolve. I wanted a taste of a much bigger city to fulfill my dreams and aspirations. After graduating Cosmetology School I knew I didn't want to move back home. I was still 18 when I finished school. I started exploring my options to move to California. As long as I got my mom's approval my possibilities were endless. To my surprise she gave me the green light to look for apartments in California. After I started doing research and looking into finding an apartment I soon realized just how expensive it was to live in California. It didn't take long for me to then decide that Atlanta was a better financial fit for my goals; plus it was only 2 hours away from home. I had everything mapped out after cosmetology school or so I thought. Needless to say, every large goal and every new level brings new challenges. I was striving to be my own boss and build a legacy, life was sure to prepare me for the life I was asking for.

I could never figure out why I worked so hard, but other people seemed to have more success than I did. As a hairstylist, I was always off on Monday so I used to go to Barnes & Nobles bookstore to read a ton of self help books. I used to always hear, "if you don't want people to know something put it in a book." I was always curious to find out what was in those books. From what I was reading, I quickly learned that CEO's don't become millionaires overnight. I had so much more to learn than I had realized. My personal life experiences had taught me so much about running a business. It taught me how to be resilient, and to never fold under pressure. I have owned two salons in my career, one with a business partner and one as a sole proprietor. I have since learned how to juggle being a wife, and a mom to two beautiful babies. I have learned to bounce back and overcome a stroke that I experienced due to pregnancy from my second c-section, this stroke resulted in immediate brain surgery. I also had to learn how to bounce back from a year after my first brain surgery to having a second brain surgery due to a brain tumor. So, please enjoy this journey with me so that you can learn how to overcome and bounce back from anything that's designed to hold you back. I want to show you how you can become resilient and bounce back from your current situation! If you believe in God and have faith the size of a mustard seed, know that God will carry you through.

BOUNCE BACK

CHAPTER 1

THE ADVERSITY ADVANTAGE

"Out of adversity comes opportunity"

I was at one one of my lowest points in my life. My husband and I packed up our apartment in Atlanta while I was seven months pregnant. During that time we also had a two year old child. Throughout my pregnancy, I was having unexplained migraines that were very extreme and painful. I could remember lying on the floor curled up in a fetal position crying on the floor. The pain was so unbearable that I could not stand, hold my head up, or even open my eyes due to the sensitivity of light. I went to the ER three times back-to-back in one week. The only thing that would work to ease the pain was morphine. On the third visit to the ER, the doctors decided to do an MRI in order to get to the bottom of what was causing my migraines. When my test results came back, my world was shaken up when I found out that I had a brain tumor. To make matters more challenging, I was seven months pregnant at the time. I was 33 years old and I didn't know exactly how to handle the weight of the news at that moment. I had never had any previous health issues and to learn that all of this was brought on due to pregnancy was mind-blowing and devastating. I was very scared and confused. I had so many unanswered questions, and the more I sat with the diagnosis the more questions I began to have. I couldn't help but wonder, "am I going to be ok?, Am I going to die?, How did this happen?, What does this mean for my unborn child?, Is it cancerous? The doctors referred me to a neurologist immediately after I gave birth. Two days before I gave birth, I learned that my sister was killed in a car accident, two days later on April 4 2017, I gave birth to our beautiful daughter Nyla by c-section. Grieving the loss of my sister and then giving birth two days later was hard. It felt like I didn't have time to grieve the loss of my sister, or get excited about the birth of my new baby because I was preparing to undergo major brain surgery. It felt like everything was happening so quickly and I didn't have time to catch my breath.

I had never experienced anything like this before in my life. Five days after leaving the hospital, we had moved from Atlanta to Birmingham. My husband and I packed everything that we could fit into our car and headed to Birmingham to start what we thought would be our new life. Adjusting at my mom's house with my husband, our two year old son and our newborn daughter; I quickly realized that I was going into a downward depression. I was completely out of my comfort zone living with my mom, dealing with postpartum depression etc. I was in a place in my life where I began to feel like a failure. To make matters worse, two weeks after giving birth, the unthinkable happened to me that shook my entire family and sent me into an even deeper depression. May 1st 2017, I was in the shower shampooing my hair. My husband was in the other room feeding our newborn, then all of a sudden, I collapsed, like the flick of a light switch. My husband must have heard the fall from in the next room. I can remember him calling my name to see if I was okay. I also remember trying to utter the word help while trying to grip the bathroom door knob, trying to get out of the bathroom and I remember collapsing again while trying to scream for help. I could not talk and no one could hear me. My husband came into the bathroom and found me lying on the floor. He was trying to hold me up in one arm while holding our daughter in the other arm. Our son was standing next to him asking, is mommy ok? He screamed out to my mother, "call 911!" My husband and my mom were both in total disbelief. He was shaking me telling me to wake up, I could not talk because my words were slurred. She whispered to him she's having a stroke! He thought I was having a heart attack. He was praying to God "please don't let me lose my wife, I need her to help me raise our kids, she's my partner and my best friend." When the ambulance arrived and did their assessments, they asked him "which hospital do you want us to take her to" UAB hospital? My husband didn't know so he said take her to the best one. As I was in the back of the paramedics truck, they continued asking me questions like "who was the president, and what year was it and I didn't know the answer to either question. Of what I can remember, when we arrived at the hospital it was like a movie scene. My husband had to wait in the waiting room and broke down into tears, scared, waiting for the doctors to come back out to tell him if his wife had died or survived. I was being immediately rushed down the hallways to the OR. While in the OR, I could remember the doctors talking to me telling me I was having a stroke, how ironic is it that it happened to be the 1st day of stroke awareness month. A blood clot had traveled through my body and went to my brain. I was completely paralyzed on my right side from head to toe. They tried to go through my head to remove the blood clot, but due to a blockage on one side of my brain they had to take an alternative route. They had to take a rod and go through my groin area to travel through my body to remove the blood clot from my brain. I later found out the doctor that was on call that day was the only doctor in the area that knew how to perform that procedure! Special thank you to Dr. Jitendra Sharma for saving my life!! I had no clue that I was under so much stress. Stress will literally kill you. You have to protect your peace at all cost from anything and anybody. Thanks to my husband for acting so quickly. When the blood clot was removed, I went into ICU for a few days of recovery and learned from the doctors that I was a walking miracle to have survived that type of stroke. I was later transported to a regular room where I had to undergo several physical therapy sessions to regain my speech back and ensure that I could walk again. I'm so thankful for my mom and aunt, they had to take care of our two week old new born and our two year old. I didn't realize just how challenging the days ahead of me were going to be mentally, physically, spiritually, and emotionally. It was an extremely emotional journey. I was having postpartum depression and trying to come to terms with what I had just experienced. I cried myself to sleep every night for over a week. I found myself being angry with God. I had so many unanswered questions. Asking God questions like "how and why did you let this happen to me? I felt like God had let me down. It was all unreal to me due to the fact that I now have to be on blood thinners the rest of my life. I had to regularly follow up with my cardiologist, neurologist, neurosurgeon, and endocrinologist. These doctor's appointments every two weeks became my new normal for a LONG time. Fast forward to September 2017, five months after the procedure; my husband and I decided to take a huge leap of faith and move back to Atlanta. We both decided that Birmingham was not a good fit for our family. He was working for USPS and I was working at UAB Hospital. We both quit our jobs. It was on a Tuesday night and we decided that we were going to pack our bags that night. Wednesday, the next morning we moved back to Atlanta. We stayed at my mother-in-law's house for two months. Then, we finally got the keys to our new apartment. The day we got our keys and moved in, I broke into tears to finally be back in my own home again. We all know that living with anyone can be very challenging. Being displaced and having to recover from grief and major surgery, I can easily say that time period of my life was the roughest five months that I had ever experienced. We had to sacrifice and go through a lot to get back to our normal life. Six months after moving into our new home, I had a doctor's appointment with my neurosurgeon. They found out that the brain tumor that they discovered had grown bigger and it was too big to be shrunk with medication. They informed me that my only option at that point was to have brain surgery again to have it removed. I found myself reliving this nightmare all over again. Here we are at brain surgery number two. It had only been a year since the first one. I immediately started to cry and ask, "God why me again?" I felt my faith being tested yet again. But then, something hit me and I started thinking why not me?

Have you ever been challenged so hard in life that you didn't understand why you were in the situation and how you would come out of it? Has life ever brought you to the brink of brokenness and made you question God and your beliefs?

When we are faced with life altering devastation, it can be nearly impossible at times to remain composed. If we're being honest, all of us at one time or another has struggled with our faith. We've all had to face some mountain of fear and then choose if we would stay there or climb over it.

How is your faith being tested right now?

What area in your life is requiring that you increase your faith and rely less on your fears?

As I prepared for my second brain surgery, one of the things that I was able to find comfort in is the fact that I had gone through the process before and survived it. Although I was fearful, I had faith knowing that I was a survivor.

When you look back over your life, how many time did you experience fear and then the very thing that you were afraid of never even happened. Fear is indeed "False Evidence Appearing Real"

Fear is a negative emotion that reduces us to our feelings. Even when you feel that things couldn't get any worse, look over your life, examine how many times you have survived hard things and KNOW that you are designed to overcome even the hardest of times.

I found a sermon that said "Don't drown in shallow waters"

To me this means that where you're standing can't take you under. If you stand in what you know and realize how far you've come, then you can see that you're closer to the finish line than you think. The water gets shallow the closer you get to the surface. You've made it through troubled waters now stand tall. Challenges tend to become greater the closer you get to your breakthrough. When I'm feeling overwhelmed, defeated, or tired I turn to my bible and read Psalms 61:2 "From the ends of the earth I call to you, I call as my heart grows faint; lead me to the rock that is higher than I. One of my favorite quotes is "When all is said and done, don't obsess over how it's not fair". "Instead, learn to live with adversity without a chip on your shoulder."

When I had a stroke at 33 years old, I was honestly very uninformed about the condition. I now find fulfillment in spreading awareness about the cost of stress along with information about the condition.

Stroke- A stroke is when blood flowing to a part of your brain is stopped either by blockage or rupture of a blood vessel.

STROKE STATISTICS:

Strokes can be fatal. 1 in every 6 deaths from cardiovascular disease was due to stroke. In the US, every 40 seconds someone is having a stroke. Every 4 minutes someone dies of a stroke. Every year more than 795,000 in the US have a stroke.

FAST

> F- Face drooping

> A- Arm weakness

> S- Speech Difficulty

> T- Time to call 911

BRAIN TUMOR - I had a pituitary adenoma. Most pituitary adenoma tumors are slow growing and benign, which means they are not cancerous and do not spread to other parts of the body. However, as they grow, they can put pressure on nearby structures, such as the nerves that connect the eyes to the brain and cause symptoms

BOUNCE BACK MOMENT:

We don't always have control over things that happen to us but there are some things that are within our control.

When faced with opposition, here are a few things that may be helpful in helping you work through hard times.

1. Honor your limits. Know when you are operating in the deficit and don't be afraid to ask for help

2. Know that there is always a lesson to be learned in every hard time. Opposition can be very painful but there is often something that can be used to push us closer to purpose.

3. Refuse to give up and remain optimistic.

https://www.brookwoodbaptistmedicalcenter.com/about/our-stories/our-stories/tnesheias-stroke-story

CHAPTER 2

RESILIENCE, RECOVERY & REDEMPTION

Weeks into recovery I started thinking to myself. My body won't be at 100% to endure the stress of dealing with clients on a daily basis, and I knew that getting back behind the chair was not possible. Just when I thought we were coming to a point of relief to finally catch a break, the transmission in our car went out right in the middle of winter. I was like Lord, I can't take this anymore. What are you trying to tell us? My husband had to walk a mile to the bus-stop to catch the bus to work for three weeks before we were able to get another car. This time our kids were 1½ and 3 years old. My son had just gotten accepted into pre-school and we didn't want him to miss out. So, my husband and I decided to make a big sacrifice. Every morning for five days a week, our family would wake up at 4:30 am to get dressed and get the kids dressed. We would drive 30 minutes across town to take my husband to work, then drive 30 minutes back across town to sit at the gas station for an hour and a half until my son's school opened up. I wasn't comfortable going back to the apartment by myself with 2 small kids in the dark. During that time sex trafficking was at an all-time high rate. So instead, I sat at the gas station in a well-lit area changing diapers in the car and feeding my kids until day break. From there, I drove 30 minutes across town in the opposite direction to take him to school and then 30 minutes back home. I had everything planned out. I would have about four hours before it was time to pick him back up. I would squeeze 1-2 clients into that 4 hour time frame, rush to pick my son back up from preschool then drive 45 minutes to my husband's job to pick him up from work. The kids and I would sit in the parking lot at his job and go to sleep in the car while we waited an hour and a half for him to get off work. We did that for a whole year until income tax time came and we got the transmission fixed on my car. I don't how I did it, but I did. At that point, I decided I would have more flexibility now because I was tired of struggling to service my clients while also struggling with my health. So, I decided, now that my car is fixed, I can let this go. There were so many things that I had in mind years ago that I wanted to do, I just didn't know how to execute those ideas. I just knew I wanted more for myself and I did not want to settle. I remember applying for social security two times to get disability and both times I got denied. I went into a slight depression for months. At some point I started to give up and thought that all I would be able to do with my life was to live on disability. I'm actually glad I got denied because deep down inside I knew that I wanted so much more out of life and I was very determined not to settle and not to give up on the life that I always dreamt about living. I had to do something to help my husband bring in more income. He was only making $11/hr feeding a family of 4 at the time. My mom lived two hours away so she would go to the food banks in her local area to stock her freezer with food once a month and we would go pick it up and bring it back to our apartment to help us with food. Even though we were getting food stamps, all of the extra still helped. So, I ended up getting a job as a waitress. While my husband worked the morning shift at his job, I had to work night shift because we had no help with our kids, so that one of us could be home with the kids who were 2 and 4 at that time. This was very hard on our family, but we had to do what we had to do in order to make it. Mentally it began to take a toll on me, getting off late nights, having to take my son to pre-school in the mornings while my daughter would homeschool with me, while I was also still trying to take clients, prepare dinner for my family, rush to pick my son up from preschool with only a 30-minute window before I had to get ready for work. After a year, it started to drain me mentally. Being resilient is absolutely crucial to maintaining good mental health. While it's totally okay to feel sad sometimes and to experience emotional pain, we don't want to mope and dwell on horrible experiences forever. One of my favorite documentaries that helped me to get back motivated is *The Secret (highly recommended)* it tells you about the law of attraction and manifestation. I was searching my mind on how I could still work and bring in income after recovery. I was always curious anyway about how to make money in my sleep. I remember what my old eyebrow tech told me years ago, "google is your best friend" (thanks Michelle)

I was always somebody who used my resources. I searched google high and low. Then I ran into a video that was talking about e-commerce. Although I had heard the word before, I didn't really know what it meant. This time I googled it. That was just what I needed to hear. It answered all of my questions.

E-Commerce- commercial transactions conducted electronically on the internet.

That was my ah ha moment. So, I began to dig deeper and ask myself, what can I sell online? What problem can I solve?. It came a little easy for me to figure it out since I was already known for specializing in hair extensions. I didn't try to reinvent the wheel. I just put my twist on what so many others had shown that had proven to work. Now, don't get me wrong, I was very hesitant to start it because I started to go through a phase of self doubt. In my mind I started thinking, now who is going to shop with me and am I really going to do well being that this market is heavily saturated? After a while, I developed an attitude of well every time I walk into the grocery store and go to the bread and chip aisle there are so many different brands literally sitting on the shelf right next to each other and none of those companies were afraid they just did it. At the end of the day, it's all about how you market and brand your product that stands out from the next in the same industry. One of my favorite business quotes is by Ronald McDonald- "take care of the customers and the business will take care of itself." I've also believed in being optimistic about anything that I do instead of being pessimistic. I believe that you attract what you think about. Being resilient means knowing how to bounce back from a painful, difficult, and overwhelming experience. Think of it as a rubber band. It can be stretched and bent a million different ways, but it still always bounces back. Pressure will cause you to bend, but never fold. We have to learn to practice self-love and self-care during this process. This isn't a one size fits all process, everyone does not bounce back the same way and just because you are less resilient does not make you less of a person. three years later, I'm still in business as the Tai Davis Collection and I'm constantly evolving.

In my research I've learned how to teach people to challenge themselves to turn a negative experience into a productive one; to counter adversity with resilience. Studies have shown that psychological resilience is the capacity to respond quickly and constructively to crisis. Also, resilience can be hard to muster for many reasons: fear, anger and confusion can paralyze us after a severe set back.

- We often blame other people for our setbacks.

- We often doubt ourselves

- Research shows that 70% of people who overcome trauma have been reported to have positive psychological growth.

Oprah Winfrey- Born in poverty in rural Mississippi to a teenage single mother. She was raped at 9 and became pregnant at 14. Her son died as an infant and now she has an award winning talk show. Her show was the highest rated in history from 1986 to 2011, and she is the ranked the richest African American of the 20th century.

Tyler Perry overcame a traumatic childhood. He had three other siblings and suffered severe abuse and molestation. He was molested by three men. But his story doesn't end there. When he was in his 20's, he saved up 12,000 and moved to Atlanta while being homeless and writing his screenplays out of his used car. On his first musical, he expected 1,200 people to come but only 30 people showed up. After that, he started missing car payments and rent, and ended up living on the street with no money. Tyler, however, didn't throw in the towel. He continued writing and working odd jobs, and in 1998, he rented out Atlanta's House of Blues to showcase, "I Know I've Been Changed" one more time. According to Biography, that's when his career took off. He started selling out tickets, and eventually had to move the show to a larger theatre. On the side, he continued writing more plays, and eventually created the popular Madea series, which was when he rose to fame.

BOUNCE BACK MOMENT:

Take some time out to acknowledge how far you have come and what you have achieved in your life.

When was the last time that you celebrated your growth? You may not be where you want to be yet, but gratitude is the gateway to abundance so appreciate your right now as you work towards what's next.

BOUNCE BACK

CHAPTER 3

LIVING YOUR TRUTH

Are you living your truth? Don't worry you are not alone. When I experienced my lowest point in life that's when it became clear to me who I was and what I stood for. It was like finding myself all over again and starting on a clean slate. I had to realize that it's ok to not always be ok. I had a lot more on my plate to juggle than I had realized. This was unchartered territory for me being a new wife with two small babies and newly developed medical conditions. I was desperately trying to figure myself out and learn the new me and manage my new life. It was much harder than I ever expected. It was not at all glamorous like I imagined it would be. Before having kids, I was always so well put together every time I walked out of my front door. After having kids, I shortly realized that it was not as easy and time was very limited. Finding time to get dressed, put on a nice pair of pumps, do a light beat face and run errands felt more like an obstacle course. I would see images of women on TV and social media who just had their babies and used to think, man how do they have the time to still look this good in hair, clothes and makeup on a daily basis? Then I had an ah ha moment and realized that someone's controlled online content could not and should not be compared to my real life. Most of these women had help through grandparents, nanny's or personal assistants. Those were snap shots and clips to "do it for the gram." I started talking to other moms who had similar backgrounds and I found that everything that I was trying to hide from was normal for being a new mom. I could remember some mornings I would forget to brush my teeth, shower and hide my new FUPA (lmbo) and literally throwing on anything to run a few errands. Then I realized I could still be cute, but not in heels, I could still have a beat face, but one that was subtle. This was the beginning stages when my mind started to shift to living more and more in my truth. I knew a few friends that drove luxury cars and lived in nice houses. I had to become okay with who I was and what I had, knowing that it's ok to not try to keep up with others because I knew that eventually my time would come. You don't have to be dependent on certain relationships to feel good about yourself, and you should never feel guilty for speaking your peace. This can go both ways, if all of your life you have lived in poverty and you have chosen to want a better life for yourself, you finally reach that level of success and want to move away from poverty and upgrade your lifestyle, then do that. Be prepared to get negative feedback like "Oh, she thinks she's better than us now". Your truth was wanting to have a better life. Remember, people may want to see you doing good, but never better than them. Also, if you want that brand new Mercedes Benz, but you know you can't afford it yet, it's ok to get a Toyota Camry or something not as expensive as the benz. The reality is, you're not going to appease everyone and that's ok. Living in your truth doesn't mean you're not good enough, it simply means that you have to own who you are and be ok with it no matter what. When you start to align yourself with who you really are, you will start to see yourself progressing more. You will start to lose people along your journey and that's ok. Stop trying to impress people that really don't even care about you. You will become more at peace with yourself when you start living out your own joy. Be a walking expression of what you feel within your soul- who you really are at the core of your values and beliefs. Your best impression of yourself is when you are not trying to make an impression. Living from your soul is living in your truth, that which will be more authentic and leave more of an impact on the people around you. It is better to discover your own truth through trial and error than to live other people's truths.

BOUNCE BACK MOMENT:

Write down your core values. This list should include all the things that you believe in and everything that you don't believe in.

Take time to prioritize doing more of the things that you feel are right and the things that make you feel good inside. Release the debilitating need to control other people's beliefs about you. What other people think of you is none of your business. Do what sets your heart on fire even if others don't believe you should.

CHAPTER 4

FINDING YOUR PURPOSE THROUGH ALIGNMENT, VISUALIZATION AND MATERIALIZATION

Finding your Purpose in life is sometimes a struggle. I truly believe in manifesting the life you want to live. You first need to change your focus. The main reason why so many people struggle with finding their purpose is because they spend too much time focusing on the problem rather than the solution. I can clearly remember googling day in and day out what it meant to find your purpose. I was searching for any and everything that would give me answers. That was until I began using manifestation as a tool to get clear on what it was that my soul came here to do. I was no longer confused, but instead it felt like something was happening inside of me. I stopped chasing my soul's purpose and instead I allowed it to come to me through the law of attraction. What I also realized in this process was that I had to change my mindset and stay focused on my goals. Sometimes, it can get a bit difficult to stay on task with our day-to-day life. Once you find out what it is that you want to do in this life write it down. Most of the time the answer that you are searching for is already dangling in our face, you are just too afraid to approach it. This is ultimately caused by our own fear. Fear is the biggest thing that will hold you back in life! Most people are afraid of finding out their purpose in life because they are too afraid of just living or letting other people project their fear on them. Worrying about what other people think and feel you should do or be will lead you into living a life of just being comfortable and not truly experiencing your full potential. People will tell you what you can't and shouldn't do because they are too afraid to live in their purpose. If you know you have a love for the human body system and care about saving people's lives, then go be a nurse or doctor. Don't let people trick you out of your spot saying I wouldn't do that because I can't stomach looking at all of that blood or they don't get paid enough for me or even more, you sure you ready for all of that studying? You know that's a lot of hard work? That is them projecting their fear onto you. Praying and asking God to make your vision plain and clear to you, He will do just that. The bible states that "You have not because you ask not." God said, "ask and you shall receive."

To have to align yourself around the right people and be intentional about everything you think and do. You have to also begin to visualize yourself in these positions in life that you desire to be in. If you are like me and like to dabble in a lot of different things and you truly love doing them all; focus on the one that makes the most sense first. Then slowly start to incorporate the other things that you love but don't overwhelm yourself.

Remember, you can have it all but not all at once.

BOUNCE BACK MOMENT:

Be intentional about surrounding yourself around new people with like minded ideas. Make a list of things you intend to be intentional about to help you get closer to your goals.

The bible tells us that, "you have not because you ask not". God said, ask and you shall receive.

James 4:2-3

CHAPTER 4

THE GOD-GIVEN VISION
(Habakkuk 2:2-3)

The Lord's Answer

> *The lord then replied: "write down the revelation and make it plain on tablets so that a herald may run with it. 3 for the revelation awaits an appointed time; it speaks of the end and will not prove false. Though it linger, wait for it; it will certainly come and not delay.*

In this chapter, I want to discuss with you the vision that God gave you. Whether that means going back to school to start a new career or adding on to the career that you already have, starting a family or whatever that vision may be. These types of ideas in life always start with an idea, a dream or a hope. God placed the vision in our pathway to give us something to work towards. How do I know its vision? It's an unshakable image or thought that won't leave your head. You will ponder on this idea and thought day and night. This is how God reminds us that He has something amazing in store for us in the future. He puts it in our mind, so that we have goals that we're working towards; no matter how many setbacks we face. These goals will come with many sacrifices and you will need to work hard, be persistent and show up for yourself consistently. God gives us supernatural energy to make things happen when you want it bad enough. There will be so many failures and setbacks that will try to block you from getting to your goals that you will need to call on God numerous times, again and again. No matter what happens, if you want to be happy and healthy.

We must learn to keep our big dreams and visions to ourselves until they manifest. Telling your big dreams and ideas to small minded people will only kill your dreams. They don't understand the process. That's why he gave you the vision and not them. When you start working on your vision you have to start surrounding yourself with like-minded people. If you are the smartest person in the circle, it's time to make some changes and surround yourself around people that are smarter than you and have similar goals in life, or those who are already going where you're trying to get to. How can you grow and expand your vision and get creative when you have a circle full of people who are content or have no desire to go further in life? These are not the people to tell your dreams too. They will always be the ones to talk you out of going after your dreams because they don't have any of their own. Don't let these people trick you out of your spot in life. These are the people that want to see you doing good, but never better than them. These are the people that root for you in your face and talk bad behind your back. Start surrounding yourself around people who think like you. Surrounding yourself with people who are positive and peaceful is so important. When I was changing and shifting my mind frame, I had to let go of those negative people in my life. I slowly had to remove myself from those people. I had to upgrade my mindset and start thinking that if you're not adding value to my life, I cannot associate myself with you. This was necessary for my growth and I can assure you that I did not regret making that decision and neither will you.

This is your life and your vision. You are in control of your life and you have to control the people in it. When you're fully ready to bring your vision to life, you have to nurture the vision like a newborn baby. It's like this, you have to do everything with intent. You have to think of it like this, when you see a beautiful flower, it didn't get that way overnight. You have to plant it, water it, and watch it grow. When you plant that seed and cover it with dirt, that's when the grit and the hard work starts. Now, you have to begin to start sowing the seeds. This is when you will be tested with many trials, tribulations, and setbacks. The moment you cover that seed with dirt, God will test your faith to see how bad you really want to see your vision manifest to reality. This will be your season to hit the ground running. You will start to build character on a whole new level. It will mean making a lot of sacrifices. The sacrifices that I choose to make are getting up at 5am to gain mental clarity, exercise, meditate, pray, and get ahead of the world before everybody starts moving and shaking. This will be a part of the grit that is required. It all boils down to how bad do you really want it? You are now beginning to water the seed that you planted. Everything may not go as planned, you will have a lot of curve balls thrown at you along this journey. People will talk bad about you, some business deals may not go as planned, you may feel scared and even start to second guess yourself. If you're not scared of your dreams, then you're not dreaming big enough. You start to develop a "I have nothing to lose" attitude and start to trust yourself then you will start to see the light at the end of the tunnel. This is where you will start to see your breakthrough manifest. Know that it doesn't happen when you think or feel it should happen. It will always happen at the appointed time. One of my favorite quotes that keep me motivated is "you have to want to succeed more than you want to breathe" by Eric Thomas a.k.a E.T. the hip hop preacher. That means getting it done by any means necessary.

BACK BOUNCE MOMENT:

Revisit your vision board, if you don't have one, create one.

Envision the life that you desire to live. Take time to gather images, quotes and other tools of inspiration to add to your board. Be sure to dream big and think of the grandest idea possible for your life?

Create a visual collage that represents your dream life. Once you're done, create an action plan that outlines the steps that you need to take in order to make your vision a reality. Your vision board will help you get a clear concept on the direction that you're going in life.

CHAPTER 6

ABANDON YOUR COMFORT ZONE

Stretch yourself by abandoning your comfort zone.

Work on yourself by committing to learning.

Take accountability and allow yourself to be held accountable.

Face your fears and be brave enough to overcome your personal limitations.

So often many of us get stuck in this space of being comfortable. Whether it be childhood friendships, careers, or even romantic relationships.

So, while growing up as a little kid I was extremely shy. As I grew into a young adult, I continued to exhibit characteristics of shyness. I moved from Birmingham, Al to Kernersville, NC only four months after graduating from high school. I have never lived away from home, let alone been away from my mom for more than a day. I was extremely nervous. I really didn't have a choice as to where I wanted to go to school or what I wanted to do as a career. The decision was made for me that I was going to Dudley Cosmetology University to become a cosmetologist because they made a lot of money and I could be my own boss. I had never lived with anyone besides my family back home. So, this was my very first experience stepping completely out of my comfort zone as a teenager. I learned that the school dorm had been shut down and we had to get an apartment plus find a roommate. The school paired us with someone close to my hometown. We had a meet and greet with the families before we moved in together. It was a completely new experience for me. Going off to school 8 hours away from home to an uncharted territory at 18 years old was definitely a stretch from my comfort zone. I cried when my mom and stepdad left after helping me get set up in school. What I didn't realize was that it was molding me into the person that I am today. Sometimes, we have to get into a space so uncomfortable to be able to reach our highest potential. So, I had to learn how to adapt around people outside of my comfort zone who I had always been so dependent on my whole life. While in cosmetology school, I was in a competition called the Chicago Midwest Beauty Show in Chicago, Il. I don't know what made me want to compete but it was for the ladies cut and color category. I knew that I wasn't the best stylist, cutter or colorist, but I wanted to compete anyway. I was hearing students around the school talk about me, even my teachers saying, "I don't even know why Lady (my nickname) is competing, she's not gonna win." Keep in mind, there were about 85 people from all over the world who had signed up for this competition. My focus was not to win, it was to simply push myself out of my comfort zone. So, I booked my flight. It was the first time I had ever rode on an airplane without my family and I was terrified. I made it to Chicago in the middle of a snow storm. My flight was delayed in the air for an extra 45 minutes so that the runway could be cleared of snow for landing. My nerves were shot to say the least; but I made it into Chicago. I was an 18 year old flying to Chicago from North Carolina alone in the middle of a snow storm and I can remember feeling like "what the hell did I just get myself into?" I had never traveled before without my family. Eventually, I was able to get settled into my hotel. That night, I decided to call one of the girls from my school to see if anybody had actually made it to Chicago. They were already there and she made a statement to me and said "oh, you actually came?" That was the moment I realized that people have been looking at me as the underdog. So, I made it to competition day. It was very intimidating to say the least. When the competition was over, I decided to hang around a bit just to see who had won. I decided to leave after they called the 3rd place winner out of 5. I was a little upset. I was walking out of the competition hall and into the hallway and they were calling the 2nd place winner and I heard my name T'Nesheia Robinson, I was like WHAT wait a minute did I just hear them right. They called my name a second time. All I remember is running back down the hallway so fast in total disbelief that I had just won 2nd place in this big competition. I remember walking up on that big stage to receive my award in front of all of those people and looking into the large crowd at the 3 girls that were from my school who didn't even place at all. My classmates and even my teachers had doubted me, but I believed in myself and it had paid off in a major way. I'll be honest, it felt good looking at their mad faces in the audience because they never thought that I could win. I felt so proud of myself for not giving up because of what other people thought about me!

So, the prize was to continue education at one of the top salons in the hair industry (Vidal Sassoon). Learning at this institution was the foundation to my career. My experience there helped me to learn so many life skills that have helped me to get where I am today. My time with the company allowed me to push myself completely out of my comfort zone and I still use those skills in my career today.

Gaining confidence in my craft and becoming more ambitious, I decided to move to Atlanta, Ga. I was only 18 but I was convinced that I could achieve anything that I set my mind to. After being out of my comfort zone for 8 months for the first time in my life, I made a lot of new discoveries about myself and about life. One thing from that experience in particular that I learned is that it gave me the courage to overcome fear. I saw myself in a completely different way and for the first time, I began to realize that life begins at the end of your comfort zone. I wanted to keep pushing myself to get uncomfortable because it was like a new journey for me. Even though it was only 2 hours away from Birmingham, I felt a little bit of a culture shock.

BOUNCE BACK MOMENT:

I want to challenge you to also abandon your comfort zone.

Take some time now to consider what it is that you can do for the first time.

Do a new thing!

Is there something you've always wanted to do, but just as quick as you get excited about it, you find a way to convince yourself to quit?

Is there a restaurant that you pass by all the time but have never tried? Have you ever tasted food from a different culture or ethnicity?

Maybe even take a different route home and actually pay attention to the world around you as you travel to your destination.

Do you find yourself preparing the same few meals?, Google a new recipe and have fun learning and tasting.

When was the last time you made an actual attempt to make a new friend? Challenge yourself to start conversations with strangers. Do you speak to the other parents at the park?

Or maybe you're bored with your current career and you could really use a few new experiences, consider getting a mentor so that you can learn something new to up your game.

CHAPTER 7

PROCESSING GRIEF

What most people don't know is that grief isn't just about death. We can grieve over a number of things. Grief is universal. At some point in everyone's life, there will be at least one encounter with grief. It can come from the death of a loved one, the loss of a job, the ending of a marriage or anything that changes your life as you know it. Grief is a very personal process to go through. There is no timeline as to when the process starts, when it ends or how to endure the process of it all because everybody does it differently. What it looks like to you may not look like that for the next person. It's important that we are mindful of this and that we allow people to grieve how they choose to without passing judgment.

Grief doesn't follow any timelines or schedules. You may cry, become angry, withdraw, or even feel empty at times. None of these things are unusual or wrong. Everyone grieves differently, but there are some commonalities in the stages and the order of feelings experienced during grief. It is a very personal process to go through, and also a very painful process. Statistics show there are 5 most common stages of grief:

> denial
>
> anger
>
> bargaining
>
> depression
>
> acceptance

Everyone won't experience all of these and it may not be in this particular order. It is different for everyone. You may experience one or many of these stages for months at a time or you may skip some of these entirely.

Stage 1 Denial- It's really hard to come to grips with what just happened. You don't want to process or you are not ready to process those overwhelming feelings and emotions. A lot of time being in denial helps us to borrow the time to process our emotions.

Examples of denial:

- Terminal illness: "this isn't happening to me, the results are wrong"

- Death of a loved one: "She's not gone, I'll see her tomorrow."

- Loss of a job: "They have it all wrong, I'm sure someone will call me tomorrow to straighten this out."

- Break up or divorce- "He's just upset right now, I'm sure we will get through this"

Stage 2 Anger- A lot of the time you misplace your anger towards the wrong people or things. You are using anger to mask the real issue. You often hide behind your anger to avoid dealing with the emotions and pain.

Examples of anger:

- Terminal Illness- "God, how could you let this happen to me?"

- Death of a loved- "How could you leave me like this, you should have taken better care of yourself."

- Loss of a job- "They had poor managers anyway."

- Breakup or Divorce- "I hate him! I hope he gets his karma"

Stage 3 Bargaining- During this phase of grief, you may find yourself having a lot of "what if" moments. What if I had done something differently? Even talks to God saying things like I promise I will do right by others if you heal my heart etc. It helps to temporarily mask the sadness, hurt and confusion.

Examples of bargaining:

- Terminal illness- "what if I would have known sooner, "if only I could have prevented this"

- Death of a loved one- "what if it was something I could have done to help?" or what if I shouldn't have said that?

- Loss of a job- maybe I should have worked more hours, or did a little more teamwork."

- Break up or Divorce- what if I should have paid him/her more attention or listen to their needs and wants.

Stage 4 Depression- this stage can feel very isolated and secluded from people and things to fully cope with the loss.

Examples of depression:

- Terminal illness- my life is about to end anyway, may as well just suffer in silence

- Death of a loved one- I cannot go in this life with him/her

- Loss of a job- I won't be able to find another job better than that one

- Breakup or Divorce- I can't live life without him/her

Stage 5 Acceptance- This does not mean that you have moved on from the grief and loss. It just means that you have accepted what life is now as you know it and you're learning to cope with the new reality of life.

Examples of acceptance

- Terminal illness- well, let me make the most of my time left with him/her and tie up some loose ends

- Death of a loved one- I'm so happy to have shared and created so many memories while I had the chance to.

- Loss of a job- maybe I should start my new business I was contemplating or find a new path in life

- Breakup or Divorce- I'm excited and nervous about what the future holds, but ultimately this was the best decision.

I have personally dealt with grief with the loss of loved ones, my marriage almost coming to an end and also dealing with my sudden health failing. This was very hard for me, but what I noticed is that I grieved very differently with each loss. The first time I experienced grief was with my grandma. This was the very first time I experienced death this close to me. It was extremely hard for me to wrap my head around the fact that she wasn't here on this earth anymore. I had grown up around her my entire life. Not to sound naive, but I was 25 when she passed away and when you're young like that all you know grandma and she's gonna always be here. It took me months to come to terms that she wasn't here anymore. I remember I could not sleep with my light off and I cried for months and I believe that was my process of dealing with it. When my Daddy passed away, we weren't that close but we were making an effort to become closer to make up for lost time with his absence from my childhood. We would talk to each other on the phone weekly making an attempt to make up for the times that we missed. We had established a pretty solid relationship for about 2 years or maybe a little more. It was a good feeling finally getting to know the other half of me for the first time in 20 something years. I was even able to build relationships with my new found siblings. My daddy and my brother had made plans to come visit me in Atlanta for my first salon opening. It was very exciting to show him who his daughter was and exactly what it is that I did as a career. I was very excited to have him spend the weekend with me. My brother called me on a Saturday morning and in my mind, I thought he was calling to tell me that they were getting ready to hit the road; but instead, he told me that my dad had passed away in his sleep overnight. I was crushed! Even though he wasn't a part of my whole life, it was still very tough to deal with losing a parent. I remember that was the very weekend that we opened and I had a full schedule full of clients. It was extremely tough because at the end of the day I was part owner of the salon so I had to push through the day and still go to work. The way our salon was setup was that we shared clients all day. My business partner was a master colorist and I was a master stylist. So, our clients had to go to her first for color then I had to finish them off with cutting and styling. That's one of the difficult parts about grief is that you still have to push through even when you feel like crawling into a hole and shutting the world out. I remember literally crying between every client that left my chair throughout my entire 8 hour shift. One of the things that I did to cope with the death of losing my daddy was getting a dog. I had never had a dog as an adult and I went back and forth about the idea of getting one, but I'm really glad that I did. It really helped me to take my mind off of losing him. It didn't take the pain away, but it helped me to distract myself from the heartache

When I had my stroke and brain tumor removal all in one year, I believe I went through all of those stages of grief again. I had so many unanswered questions and I felt like God had let me down in a major way. I was angry at God for a long time.

The takeaway - no one person will grieve the same as the next person. It will look and feel different from person to person. There is no time limit and you may not experience every stage of grief and some people do. You can also be stuck on one stage of grieve for weeks, months or years. If you ever feel stuck and can't cope, I would urge you to seek professional help.

They have online, phone and in person help.

Mental health Hotline # 1-800-662- HELP 4357
www.samhsa.gov

BOUNCE BACK MOMENT:

1. Seek a professional therapist

2. Talk through and work through your fears, traumas, triggers and grief with a trusted professional.

3. Rekindle a hobby that once brought you joy and fulfillment, or find a new hobby that allows you to be creative.

4. Adopt a pet

5. Watch a few good comedy movies (laughter is good for the soul)

CHAPTER 8

WEIGHT LOSS

Whew Chile…. Can we get into this weight loss talk? I'm sure most of you like myself have struggled with losing weight. When most of us look at ourselves in the mirror we don't like what we see. You know what I'm talking about? Those sideways turn in the mirror, sucking in the gut, or that extra chin fat right? We lose the weight and gain it back. It's like an emotional roller coaster ride. I'm sure most of you, like me, must have tried all kinds of weight loss diets and still couldn't seem to keep the weight off. It's time to take back control over our bodies and start caring for our bodies the proper way with the right foods to nurture it, so that you can become healthy, slimmer and a more vibrant you.

In today's society we as women are becoming much busier. We are becoming entrepreneurs, we are raising babies, some of us still have our 9-5 occupations and we're juggling side hustles. Now, since most of us are working from home, and trying to survive during this global pandemic, you have 2 choices to come out of quarantine really rounded or really fit. People are facing death so don't beat yourself up because you have gained a few pounds. Let's take a moment to see why you are gaining weight. If you are like me there is this thing called emotional eating. I'll eat literally for any and all reasons. I'll eat when I'm happy, sad, stressed, celebrating or just for no damn reason at all simply because I just love food. Lol. Luckily in today's society, we don't even need to leave our home to hire a personal trainer or to workout at all. There are so many ways to work out from the comfort of our homes. There is now access to all types of virtual fitness groups and virtual coaches. But I get it, some of you like to get motivated by working out in a gym or running outside. No matter what type of eater you are (emotional eater, unconscious eater, habitual eater, critical eater, sensual eater, or energy eater) I'm sure you can agree that it all contributes to weight gain right?

I think the most common eaters are emotional eaters as I just mentioned.

So, now that we have identified the types of eaters, how do we fix this problem? So, let me just say I'm no fitness expert, but I do speak from trial and error and personal experience. First things first. You have to change your mindset about how you view food and weight loss. Everything is mental. It's not about just losing the weight to look good, but it also becomes a lifestyle change. Studies show about 95% of American's who lose weight gain it right back within 3 to 5 years. You have to train your mind to eat for health and not always personal gratification, now I'm not saying that you can't enjoy a night out with friends, or family. But it all comes down to eating in moderation. I'm not saying this will be easy, but it will require you to be mentally focused and dedicated. I'm not telling you to throw everything in your refrigerator away, but you can start to modify it. A rule of thumb that I stick to when grocery shopping is to shop for food outside of the aisle.

Meaning stay away from food that's on the shelves because it's packed with preservatives. It's good to stock up on fresh fruits, vegetables, and protein or seafood of your choice. However, keep in mind that dairy foods may keep you bloated like milk cheese, etc. I suggest that you develop some sort of routine that fits your daily schedule with eating and working out.

Train your mind to not eat for instant gratification, but for the health benefits in the long run. A way to help with doing that is to plan your meals out. For instance, whatever your free day is during the week. Use that day to prep your meals for the week (breakfast, lunch, dinner, and snack). Get creative, mix it up and make it fun! Meal prepping is one sure way to help portion control, overeating, and staying away from those tempting fast food drive through for a quick fix. It also promotes healthy weight loss. Change your mindset on how you think about food. Eating to live is what I think about when I eat. When you're able to grasp that concept that's when you know you're on the path to making this lifestyle change. I also like to incorporate and challenge myself to detox and do lots of green smoothies to cleanse my body. Also keep in mind that it's a combination of working it and eating the right food. One of my best weight loss regimens helped me lose 30 lbs in 6 weeks. No fad diets, no diet pill, just strictly hard work, being consistent and dedicated. A lot of people ask how I was able to do that? I made a choice to make a lifestyle change and I got tired of losing and gaining. I completely changed my eating habits. I cut out anything that I could think of, fried and white. What do I mean by white? Anything that consisted of sugar, flour, and starchy foods. So potatoes, juice, bread, rice. Rice was the hardest for me. I grew up in the south, so most of our meals consisted of some type of rice, smothered meat and gravy. I started making a more conscious decision of the food I put on my mouth. Everything I ate was intentional. I had to learn how to try new and healthier foods despite the taste because I knew it was healthy for me. I began to workout daily and that consisted of at least 45 minutes of cardio daily at least 5 days a week. I also had a personal trainer, but we never used a gym. That taught me that you don't need a gym to workout. My favorite go to for workouts now is what I call "YouTube University" lol, you can literally tailor a whole workout to your needs from beginner to intermediate while working out in the comfort of your own home. It also helps to take pictures and document your journey. If you have access to an accountability partner that helps out a whole lot! Just make sure you have a partner that wants to lose the weight and eat healthy just as much as you do and someone that's dependable and consistent. Document your process week by week to see your progression. They say anything that you do over 30 days becomes a habit. The same way you plant the seed and manifest every other area of your life you have to take the same approach about making this journey a lifestyle change. You have to know that you got this in the bag. You can do this, take pictures to remind yourself of how far you have come and where you're never going back to.

Let's get to the reason why you are gaining weight and why when you get it off it won't stay off. Studies show from everydayhealth.com that there are 9 contributing factors that cause unintentional weight gain.

- Your Body Works Against You

- There Are No Quick Fixes

- Exercise Can't Conquer All

- Diet Supplements Don't Work

- Fad Diets Don't Work for Long

- One Diet Doesn't Fit All

- Cardio Is Essential (and Strength Training Helps Too)

- He Can Eat More Than She Can

- It's Not a Diet, It's a Lifestyle Change

BOUNCE BACK MOMENT

Challenge yourself to do Cardio for 30 minutes 3-4 times a week

YouTube had great free workout videos, I highly recommend them. One of my favorite YouTube workout videos to keep me going and losing weight is Keaira Lashae.

CHAPTER 9

BOUNCE BACK FROM DIVORCE OR A BAD RELATIONSHIP

I'm sure most of us have been through a bad break-up or divorce right? The death of a relationship is never an easy thing to deal with. This is another part of grief that I talked about previously. It can be a very painful experience. It's a very hard place to be in. When you have spent years of building a life together with someone now you have to try to adjust to what your new normal is. I know it's hard and easier said than done, but know it's time to embrace the gifts that endings bring. You have to learn how to focus on what's ahead instead of all the fusing, pointing fingers, and blaming. By doing this it makes it that much harder to move forward. It's not going to be an easy journey, but you can at least start somewhere with these small things. Learning how to gain control of your emotions, indulge in them, let them go then get on with your life. Doing this will show you that you have control of your life, not your emotions. You and your ex may have disagreements for a while on who was wrong or right, remember that is just a point of view and everyone is entitled to it. That doesn't mean that it's right or wrong. Be careful who you vent to and allow to have an opinion on your marriage or relationships breakup. Everyone, even those that are on your side may have an agenda good or bad and their own perspective based on their experiences that may not necessarily be relevant to you or your situation. Don't allow yourself to be so easily influenced by the options or advice of others including professional help. Rather just take in the information, dissect it, and do what feels right for you. Now you can begin to try to find peace in the ending of your relationship or marriage, it's time to focus on things that are important for you not to lose yourself along the way. The best way to bounce back is not to focus so much on the past at this point. You have got to do things that make you feel happy again despite the hurt, anger, and pain that you feel. First things first, self love and self care. It's so easy to get caught up in the emotions and the hurt that we tend to lose ourselves in the midst of it. Get back to the essence and the core of what makes you happy. If it's a hot bath while the kids are sleeping with your favorite glass of wine to de-stress, listening to your favorite songs to lift your spirits, retail therapy or having lunch with a girlfriend for a few good laughs then do just that. However this may look to you. It's very necessary to get back on track to being the best you. Taking the time of getting to know you all over again should be fun and exciting. You're not so consumed with trying to lose yourself in another person's joy. Oftentimes as wives or girlfriends we tend to lose ourselves and things become all about what our spouse or significant other likes and wants. This is the perfect time to shift the focus back on yourself. I know a new relationship may be a bit far fetched right now (or maybe not) but take time to genuinely love yourself with no interruptions. This will also be a good time to rekindle some old career interests or hobbies. If you put your career on hold maybe because it was best for the family or to help your husband run the business now is the perfect time to get your career path back on track at least now you will have help with the kids while you're in school. This will also keep your mind preoccupied and not focus so much on your divorce or break up

BOUNCE BACK MOMENT:

Write down a list of things you put on hold during your marriage/relationship and gradually find your way back to making those things happen.

CHAPTER 10

STORIES OF WOMEN WHO HAVE EXPERIENCED A BOUNCE BACK

For me the hardest thing I ever experienced was my mom's 2nd diagnosis of cancer which resulted in her passing. It felt as though her initial healing was taken for granted in a way and I was front row as her health deteriorated and the last 6 months of her life.

A few of the ways I have managed the pain of grief

1. Sought professional help. I initially found a licensed therapist to support caring for a terminally ill parent. I had never been through before and really wanted to process my emotions, the realities, and still sustain my faith that God's will prevailed. I found a counselor that shared the same faith as

me and they are still a key integral part of my life 5 years later.

Interestingly 1 week I started counseling, my mom died. So we immediately transitioned into grief counseling. I am no longer afraid to ask for help in any areas of my life as a result of seeking mental health support services.

2. I focused on my holistic health. This is inclusive of my general practitioner, ob gyn, therapist, and acupuncturist. I made sure that I created a community of health professionals that I could rely on for my own health needs.

3. I went after one of my BIG goals. For 10 years, I talked about going to graduate school. About 9 months after my mom passed I responded to an email from Regent University that they were waiving application fees. Within 8 days of that call, I was on a conditional acceptance and in class. The growth I experienced was amazing. I grew new skills and have even moved in the direction of coaching full time which I got my degree in.

4. I start my days expressing gratitude. Prior to all of this, I would start my day usually scrambling to get to work and get the kids to school. I am now much more grounded to express gratitude before doing anything.

5. I share my story. I am not ashamed to share that while I am saddened by my mom's death, I have trusted God in this process. My hope is that God's love and Jesus' redemption is present in the story.

-Lynette Phillips

My journey begins post-graduation from the University of Alabama. As a college graduate, I was able to check-the-box concerning having a college degree. However, I was not confident in my direction and purpose in my field of study which was Healthcare Management. The initial career opportunities granted some exposure to different positions in the field, but it was so broad that it did not provide a clear road map to establish what I wanted to pursue. The following steps were taken to determine the best career path for my life:

1. Be Open to Different Opportunities – Some career opportunities were in different field(s) which was acceptable and did not diminish my college degree in a different field. In fact, it created the platform to explore more employment opportunities in different sectors. Some were great and others were not.

2. Learn New Skills – New skills obtained from different positions have been transferrable and have had the right impact at the right time.

3. Ask God to Reveal Your Purpose – HE answered my prayer and led me to higher education. Game on! I discovered that I loved working with adult learners who have a desire to obtain an associate's, bachelor's, or master's degree.

4. Expect to Be Pushed to a New Level – Returning to school to obtain a Master of Business Administration degree became a resounding bell in my ear. God strategically delivered numerous signs for me to turn to school that I could not ignore. I obeyed his command and enrolled in the MBA

program offered at the university I worked for. Four months later, I was informed that I would be a part of a system-wide layoff. But look at God's work, HE knew I needed to be actively enrolled in an advanced degree program to prepare for the doors HE would only open for me. I transitioned into a new role at another college about seven months later, while I was still in my program.

5. Relocation Allows You to Level Up – Explore career opportunities in different cities and/ or states. I found that I have been able to advance my career by being flexible to relocate to areas that fall outside of metropolitan areas. The rewards have been great which include advancement, training, and salary increases.

-Leah R. Fields

Every woman has situations that can either make them or break them. I am Shannica Allen-Dowdell and I have struggled for years with accepting the woman that I am. There were times when I was called names such as ugly, popeyes wife, and skinny meg which are all considered to be derogatory names. What I saw in my mirror was masculine features such as big hands, strong features, big feet, and my height which was not the norm. These incidents have caused me to struggle with my self-esteem for years. Looking in the mirror sometimes caused me to cry because I could not see what others saw. It took me a very long time to see that no matter how others felt about me I had to build confidence within myself.

The woman that I have become is known to be a "Superwoman". I have had to learn how to face my fears, my inconsistencies, and the things that caused my many insecurities. There are six things that I did to bounce back to be the woman that I was created to be.

1. I began having a relationship with GOD. Long talks shed many tears because I didn't know where to start. I poured my heart out to GOD and asked for his help. As I became faithful with our relationship I started to see change.

2. I considered seeking professional help but in the midst, I realized that I was my own enemy. I never

understood the importance of self-talk and affirmations. I highly recommend this action because it works.

For Ex: I am Beautiful, I am a Queen, I must not settle for anything that I do not want, and I am more than ENOUGH.

2. I focused on wearing smaller shoes so to counter that insecurity I fell in love with a fetish for shoes of all different types, colors, and styles. I began embracing all of the attributes that caused me to be considered different. Now I receive compliments when I am all dolled up.

3. Along with my aspirations, I began to look at myself differently and set goals that I know that I had to strive and work towards. To make that goal a reality I would put a date on it and then go hard to make it happen. This is biblical everyone, the Lord answered me, and said, Write the vision, and make it plain upon tables, that he may run that readeth it. Habakkuk 2: 2. So I continue to do this. On January 4, 2018, I publicly sent a dear husband message on social media just to test the verse on a

bigger scale. I met my charming prince on February 18, 2018, on January 4, 2021, we got married and intend to live happily ever after.

4. I started to listen to and read self-help and motivational videos. This boosted my thinking and my ability to envision myself as my hero. The more I did this, the more I realized and believed that there is nothing wrong with me. I started to water the flower in me and as I did that I watched myself grow.

5. I surrounded myself with positive individuals, sought mentors in areas that I wanted to master, and created an environment called Heels & Ties to Success Empowerment Group to learn from other men and women who may have similar struggles. This helped me not only to grow but to overcome and recognize that I am only "Human". I changed my perspective and that changed my narrative. Now I am my own Superwoman and I am loving me because I am more than enough.

My Truth,

Shannica Allen-Dowdell

SUMMARY

You can bounce back from anything you put your mind to. Although, it won't be easy and yes, it's going to take a lot of grit and hard work, but as long as you still have blood running through your veins anything is possible. To my entrepreneurs going through this tough time in this pandemic. We are all feeling the raft of it. This is when you truly have to learn and know what it means to pivot. You have to know shift gears and learn how to re-strategize. If you have a brick and mortar that you have to close down don't look at it as the end of your business. This is now an opportunity for you to pivot and now think of a strategy for e-commerce (online sales) One of the biggest things that made an impact on my business due to covid-19 was right when I released my hands on 1:1 wig making class, and students signed up. I had to shut it all down and give refunds. So I had to pivot and make digital content and take my classes digital. It won't always be easy, but enough hard work, being consistent and being dedicated to the tasks at hand, then you're on your way to bouncing back. My favorite quote from Ronald McDonald- take care of the customers and the business will take care of itself. I have since started my Wig line, I've introduced hair care products to my brand and my husband and I started a business in real estate - Property Preservation, where we maintain bank owned foreclosed homes. If I can bounce back from adversity what's stopping you? I believe in you! But most importantly, you have to believe in you!

ABOUT THE AUTHOR

T'Nesheia Davis is from Birmingham, Al. As a little girl she was always a dreamer and never wanted to settle which is why she moved to Atlanta, Ga at the age of 18. Which for most would have been frightening at that age coming from a small town but she always grabbed fear by the horns. She always new that she wanted to help people, whether being a nurse, or being a cosmetologist. After high school she went to to study Cosmetology In Kernersville, North Carolina where she graduated from Dudley Cosmetology University. She always knew that people looked at her as being a underdog but she never let that stop her drive. She is recognized in the beauty industry as a hairstylist and educator. She has held her licensed over 19 years. She has since retired from behind the chair due to her medical history. While Tai has retired from styling hair behind the chair she is still very much involved and influential with the beauty industry. She has since mastered the art of wig making. She also enjoy teaching other entrepreneurs how to grow their business and growing to the next level of success. She has recently started her own hair care line Tai Davis Collection which is doing very well while working along her husband with a new business called property preservation which is maintaining bank owned foreclosed homes. Needless to say she didn't let her adversities slow her down and she was able to bounce back from 2 medical crisis.

Tai Davis Featured in local media for her miraculous medical results.

https://www.brookwoodbaptisthealth.com/services/stroke-treatment/our-stories/tnesheias-stroke-story